What's Cooking?

By Patty Michaels
Illustrations by Clarice Elliott

Ready-to-Read

SIMON SPOTLIGHT • An imprint of Simon & Schuster Children's Publishing Division • New York Amsterdam/Antwerp London Toronto Sydney New Delhi • 1230 Avenue of the Americas, New York, New York 10020 • This Simon Spotlight edition January 2025 • Illustrations copyright © 2025 by Clarice Elliott • All rights reserved, including the right of reproduction in whole or in part in any form. • SIMON SPOTLIGHT, READY-TO-READ, and colophon are registered trademarks of Simon & Schuster, LLC. For information about special discounts for bulk purchases, please contact Simon & Schuster Special Sales at 1-866-506-1949 or business@simonandschuster.com. • The Simon & Schuster Speakers Bureau can bring authors to your live event. For more information or to book an event contact the Simon & Schuster Speakers Bureau at 1-866-248-3049 or visit our website at www.simonspeakers.com. • Manufactured in the United States of America 1124 LAK • 2 4 6 8 10 9 7 5 3 1 • Library of Congress Cataloging-in-Publication Data • Names: Michaels, Patty, author. | Elliott, Clarice, illustrator. • Title: What's cooking / by Patty Michaels ; illustrations by Clarice Elliott. • Description: New York : Simon Spotlight, 2024. | Series: Kids around the world | Summary: "What's cooking in the kitchen? In this book, readers will learn about how ingredients from across the sea end up on their plates, how similar dishes were invented in different countries, and what sweet treats kids enjoy for special occasions. Gather around the table for a delicious journey around the world!"—Provided by publisher. • Identifiers: LCCN 2024039421 (print) | LCCN 2024039422 (ebook) | ISBN 9781665963435 (hardcover) | ISBN 9781665963428 (paperback) | ISBN 9781665963442 (ebook) • Subjects: LCSH: Cooking—Juvenile literature. • Classification: LCC TX652.5 .M397 2024 (print) | LCC TX652.5 (ebook) | DDC 641.5—dc23/eng/20240923 • LC record available at https://lccn.loc.gov/2024039421 • LC ebook record available at https://lccn.loc.gov/2024039422

Glossary

al dente: something cooked just enough to retain a firm texture

condiment: something that enhances or adds flavor to a dish

cuisine: a style of cooking or preparation of food

culinary: a word related to cooking in a kitchen

cultivated: something that has been prepared or raised for harvest

fermentation: a process by which microscopic organisms like fungi or bacteria break down sugars to result in various foods or products

forage: to search or seek for provisions

fungus: a group of organisms that produce spores and feed on dissolved organic matter

ingredients: a part of any combination or mixture

kimjang: an annual traditional process of preparing and sharing large quantities of kimchi

Mardi Gras: a festive day typically celebrated in New Orleans, Louisiana, before the start of the Lenten season leading up to Easter

microbes: very small living things

umami: a taste sensation that has a rich or savory flavor characteristic

Note to readers: Some of these words may have more than one definition. The definitions above match how these words are used in this book.

Contents

Chapter 1:
Recipe for Success 4

Chapter 2:
Same but Different 14

Chapter 3:
Time for Cake! 24

Become a Chef! 32

Note to readers: Every region has its own unique cuisine. These are just some of the delicious dishes that people enjoy around the world.

Chapter 1: Recipe for Success

What's cooking around the world?

Every region and community has its own unique ingredients, dishes, and **cuisine** (say: kwuh-ZEEN). Let's embark on a delicious **culinary** (say: KUH-li-nair-ee) adventure around the globe!

Every recipe starts with basic **ingredients** (say: in-GREE-dee-ents). Many regions around the world have unique ingredients that make their recipes even more delicious!

In Italy, white truffles are sometimes grated over dishes like pasta to add an **umami** (say: ooh-MAH-me) flavor.

White truffles are a kind of **fungus** that grows underground by certain types of trees in forests near Alba, Italy.

Dogs and pigs are specially trained to **forage** (say: FOR-ij) for truffles because of their excellent sense of smell.

In countries like Japan and South Korea, and on an island in Russia called Sakhalin (say: SA-ka-leen), a **condiment** (say: CON-duh-mint) called wasabi (say: wuh-SAH-bee) is very popular.

Wasabi is a plant that comes from the mustard family.
It is grated into a paste that is green in color and very spicy!

We've had a taste of umami and spicy flavors. How about sweet? The vanilla bean was first **cultivated** (say: KUL-tuh-vay-tid) in Mexico more than six hundred years ago.
It is added to tasty desserts like ice cream and cakes.

Another popular sweet ingredient is sugar, which comes from the sugarcane plant. This plant was first cultivated in New Guinea around ten thousand years ago. Today, sugarcane is most commonly turned into table sugar.

Chapter 2:
Same but Different

Around the world and across time, people have created similar dishes in different ways. For example, do you like spaghetti?
How about instant noodles?
Pasta and noodles are similar, but different!

Pasta can be made into different shapes and sizes and is typically boiled until **al dente** (say: al DEN-tay) and served covered in sauce. Noodles can be served deep-fried, stir-fried, or in soups.

Dumplings are also made in many ways around the world. Khinkali (say: heen-KAHL-lee) are dumplings originating from the country of Georgia. They are filled with broth and meats or vegetables.

Originating in China, dim sum is a traditional breakfast or lunch meal consisting of various dumplings and other small dishes.

Rice is a staple food in many places around the world and can also be prepared in various ways.

Thieboudienne (say: CHE-boo-JEN) is the national dish of Senegal. It is a traditional meal made of rice, fish, vegetables, and spices.

In Vietnam, cơm tấm (say: come-TAHM) is a dish made with rice grains that have been broken during the milling process.

Mango sticky rice is a Southeast Asian dessert that is made with glutinous rice, mango slices, and coconut milk.

Many foods around the world are made by a process called **fermentation** (say: fur-men-TAY-shun).

When yeast, a type of fungus, is added to a mixture of flour and water, the resulting dough ferments and rises. Once the dough is baked, it becomes bread, a common food around the world!

Kimchi (say: KIM-chee) originated in Korea and is also a fermented food. It consists of various pickled vegetables. Every year, many communities gather to make kimchi in a process called **kimjang** (say: KIM-jahng).

Some types of cheeses are made by fermenting milk with **microbes** (say: MY-krowbz) like yeast, mold, or bacteria to develop the flavors. People across the world have been making cheese for over seven thousand years!

Chapter 3:
Time for Cake!

There is always room for cake! In the United States, it is common to serve a special cake lit with candles on someone's birthday. Birthday celebrations with cake and candles originated in Germany and were called Kinderfeste (say: KIN-der-fehst).

Other cakes are served around the world to celebrate different holidays. In Japan, a cake called kagami mochi (say: ka-ga-MEE mo-CHEE) is a sweet rice cake eaten for New Year's celebrations.

A dessert called a king cake is a popular treat in Louisiana during **Mardi Gras** (say: MAR-dee grah). Inside the cake hides a small figurine. Whoever receives the slice with the figurine in it is considered lucky!

In France, a dessert called a bûche de Noël (say: BOOSH dih no-ELL) is served to celebrate Christmas. It looks like a yule log! The "log" is topped with candy mushrooms and berries, and has brown frosting that resembles tree bark.

Pavlova (say: PAV-loh-vah) is a popular cake in Australia and New Zealand that is served at Christmastime. Because Christmas occurs during the summer in the southern hemisphere, the pavlova is a refreshing treat!

In China, a pastry called a mooncake is served to celebrate the Mid-Autumn Festival. These cakes can be made with different flavors and fillings.

Wasn't that a delicious adventure?

Different foods from around the world are not only tasty, but they also bring people together to celebrate unique cuisines everywhere.

Become a Chef!

Now that you've learned about different ingredients and dishes from around the world, let's create your own special dish!

You will need:

- **a grown-up to help you**
- **construction paper in different colors**
- **scissors**
- **paper plate**
- **glue**
- **crayons or markers**

1. Draw various ingredients on construction paper. What ingredients would go well in your dish? Is it a sweet or savory meal?
2. Cut out your ingredients with the help of a grown-up.
3. Glue your ingredients onto a paper plate.
4. Decorate your dish with crayons or markers.
5. Serve your meal!

Bon appétit (say: BOHN ah-PEH-tee)!